All rights reserved. First published in
the United States in 1986 by Platt & Munk,
a division of Grosset & Dunlap.
Grosset & Dunlap is a member of
The Putnam Publishing Group, New York.
Originally published in Great Britain in 1986
by Walker Books Ltd., London.

Printed in Italy.

Library of Congress Catalog Card Number: 86-80516
ISBN 0-448-10831-3 A B C D E F G H I J

My First Book of
WORDS

illustrated by
Julie Lacome

Platt & Munk, Publishers • New York
A Division of Grosset & Dunlap

CONTENTS

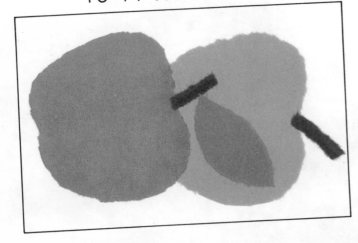

18-19 On the Street

20-21 At the Beach

22-23 On the Farm

24-25 At Work

26-27 Animals

28-29 Colors

30-31 A Word Game

My Body

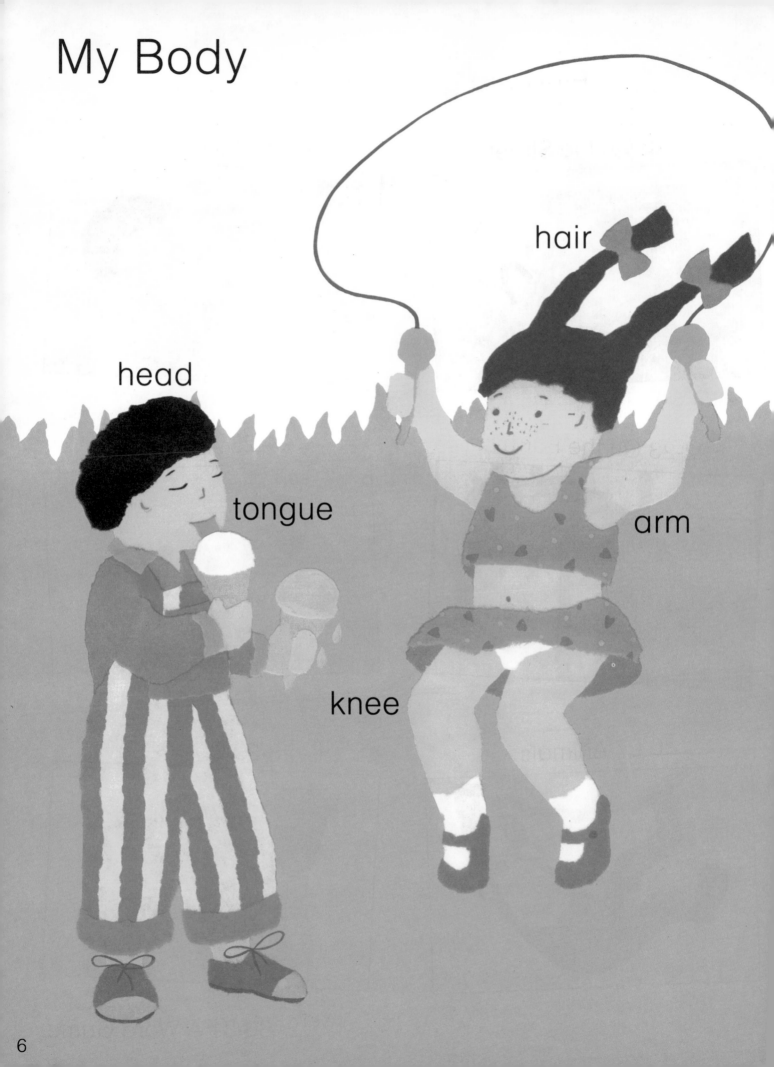

Find the boys.
Find the girls.

hand

elbow

shoulder

tummy

bottom

leg

foot

What I Wear

socks

dress

T-shirt

sweater

shoes

pants

What are you wearing?

pajamas

hat

shorts

shirt

jeans

boots

What I Eat
What do you like to eat?

bread

carrots

bananas

jam

cupcake

tomatoes

eggs

peas

cookie

fish

cheese

cherries

orange juice

apples

hamburger

What I Do

run

read

cry

splash

dance

drink

eat

swing

fall

laugh

jump

sleep

14

In the House

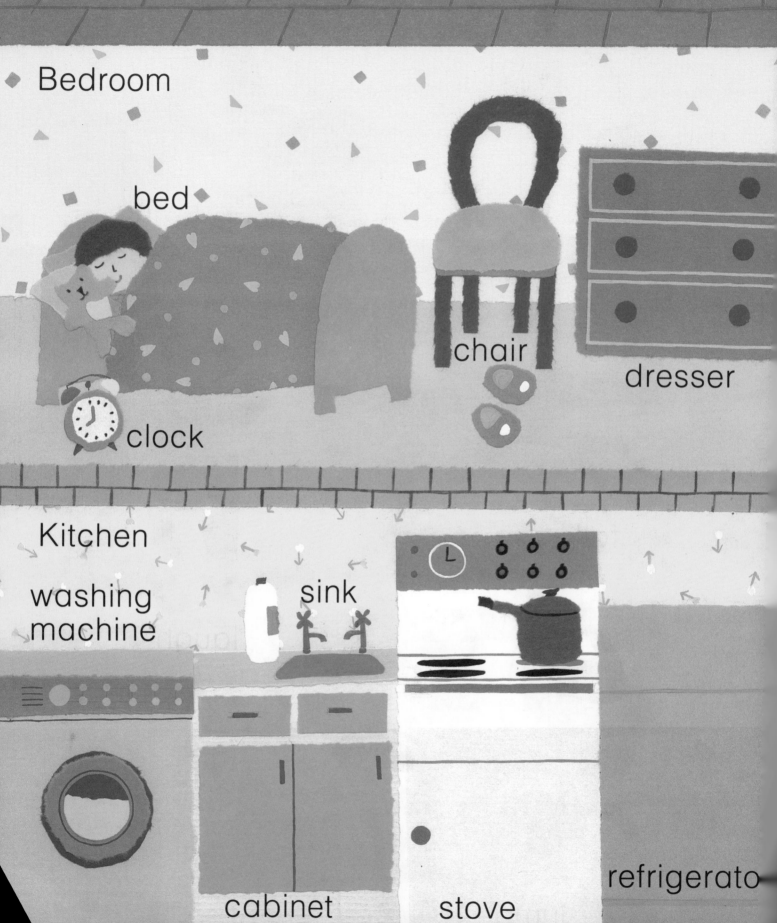

Bedroom

bed

chair

dresser

clock

Kitchen

washing machine

sink

cabinet

stove

refrigerato

Who is sleeping?

Bathroom

shower

sink

toilet

bathtub

Living room

picture

lamp

television

sofa

The Toy Shop

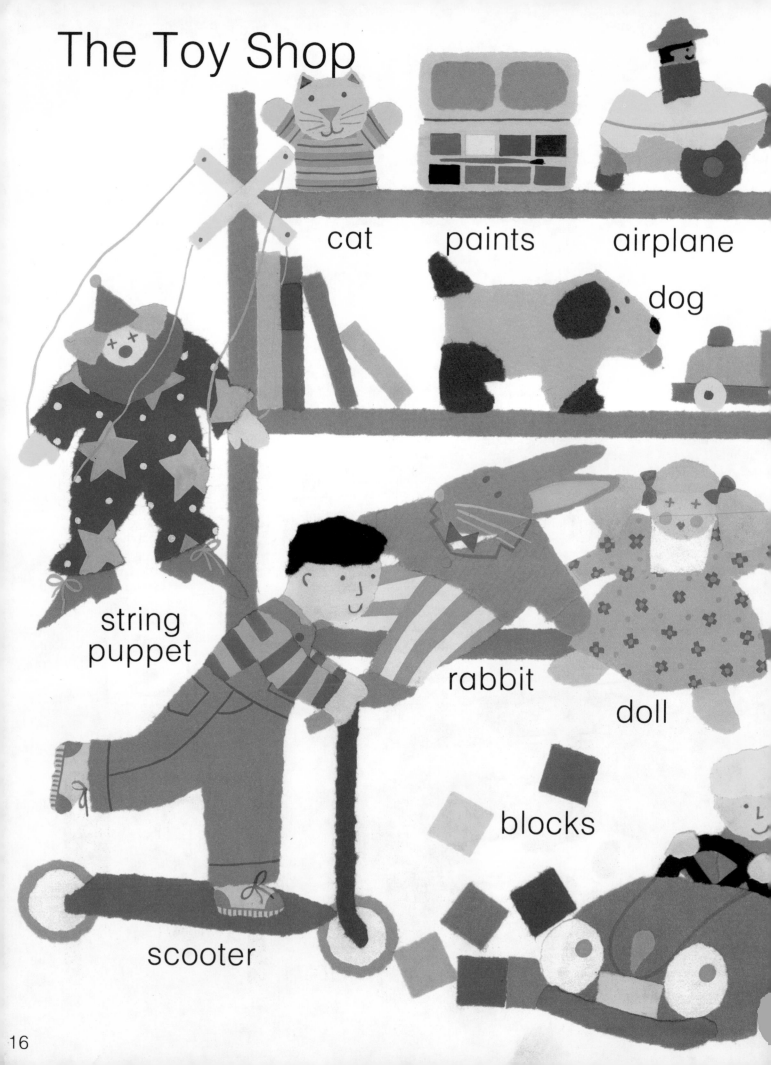

cat

paints

airplane

dog

string puppet

rabbit

doll

blocks

scooter

ball

tiger

yo-yo

train

hand
puppet

rocking horse

robot

pedal car

teddy
bear

On the Street

tricycle

motorcycle

car

store

tree

sidewalk

bus

bicycle

pickup truck

At the Beach

boat

kite

sun

flag

sun hat

ice cream

sand castle

beach ball

seashells

pail

shovel

swim tube

umbrella

beach chair

ocean

towel

beach bag

crab

picnic

starfish

On the Farm

apple trees

ducks

pond

hens

farmer

cow

dog

pig

23

At Work

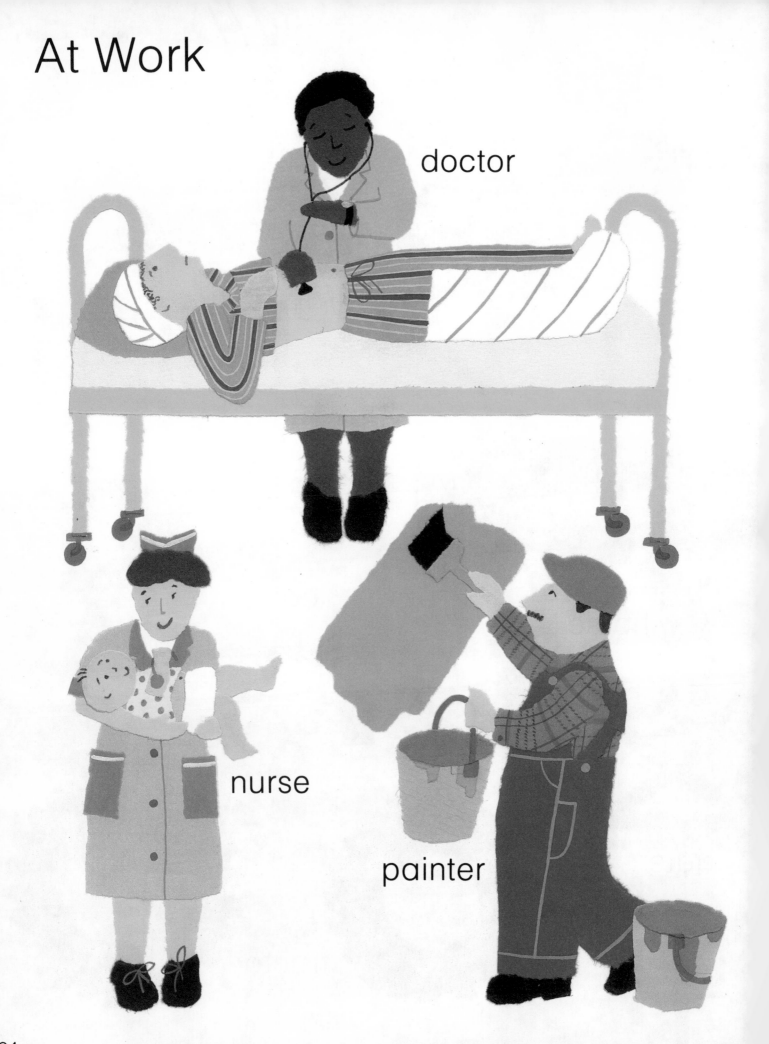

doctor

nurse

painter

repairman

cook

builder

veterinarian

Animals

monkey

butterfly

lion

raccoon

camel

elephant

crocodile

snake

turtle

parrot

bear

tiger

giraffe

hippopotamus

Colors

Find these colors in the picture.

pink   blue   orange   white   green

gray   red   yellow   black   purple

A Word Game

Find a picture for each of these words.

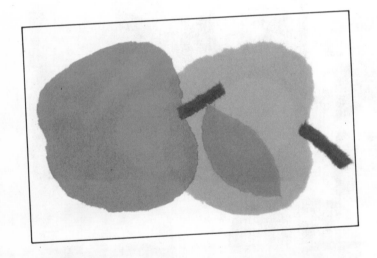

truck   monkey   horse   dress
swing   eat   pigtail   robot
apples   painter   pot   pencil